W9-BRZ-224

6.95
o/o

FRISBEE® DISC FLYING is for me

FRISBEE® DISC FLYING is for me

text and photographs by
Tom Moran

 Lerner Publications Company   Minneapolis

This book was prepared under the supervision of John "Dreamer" Weyand, member of the 1976 United States Frisbee Disc All Stars and current member of the Flapjack-Guts championship team. Weyand is noted as the innovator of the upside-down "Dream" throw. The author wishes to give him special thanks for his invaluable assistance and courtesy. The author would also like to thank Dan Roddick and the International Frisbee Disc Association and the organizers of the World Championship Beach Flying Disc Tournament.

Photographs on pages 30 (top) and 40 by Larry La Sota Photography. Photograph on page 39 (bottom) courtesy of John Weyand.

The use of the trademark FRISBEE in this book is with the permission of and under license from Wham-O Manufacturing Company, 835 East El Monte Street, San Gabriel, California. FRISBEE is a registered trademark of Wham-O Manufacturing Company, U.S. Trademark Reg. No. 679,186 issued May 26, 1959, for toy flying saucers for toss games. References in the title and text of this book to FRISBEE and FRISBEE discs and saucers are intended to be and are limited solely to the disc products manufactured and sold by Wham-O Manufacturing Company under the trademarks FRISBEE, SUPER PRO FRISBEE, MINI FRISBEE, FASTBACK FRISBEE, PRO MODEL FRISBEE.

LIBRARY OF CONGRESS CATALOGING IN PUBLICATION DATA

Moran, Tom.
   Frisbee disc flying is for me.

   (A Sports for me book)
   Summary: A disc-flying expert gives a group of children lessons in throws, catches, stunts, and special flying disc games.
   1. Flying discs (Game)—Juvenile literature.
[1. Flying discs (Game)] I. Title. II. Series.
GV1097.F7M67   796.2   82-244
ISBN 0-8225-1137-1   AACR2

Manufactured in the United States of America

International Standard Book Number: 0-8225-1137-1
Library of Congress Catalog Card Number: 82-244

1　2　3　4　5　6　7　8　9　10　91　90　89　88　87　86　85　84　83　82

Hi! My name is Trav, and this is my friend Alex. She is my age and lives near my home. Our favorite sport is throwing and catching Frisbee® flying discs. We love to watch them soar through the air. We can throw them so high that they become small dots in the sky. A few moments later, they glide smoothly back to the ground.

Most flying discs look like upside-down saucers. The top of the disc is called the **flight plate**. Often there are several circles called **flight rings** formed into its surface. If you look at the disc from its side, you will see that it has a slightly domed shape. The curve along the outside edge is called the **shoulder**. The bottom edge is called the **rim**.

Flying discs are inexpensive and will last a long time. There are hundreds of different kinds. Frisbee® flying discs are made by one company, and other companies make other kinds. Flying discs come in many sizes, shapes, and colors. I enjoy trying as many different kinds as I can.

Some of the more unusual discs are called **novelty discs**. Some glow in the dark, and others make funny noises as they sail through the air. Some novelty discs have strange shapes or have domes, pyramids, or handles on them. Other discs are very thin and have no center. These discs can be thrown very far.

Some discs are very small, about the size of my hand. Because they are also lightweight, they are safe for indoor play if you are careful. They can be thrown or snapped between your fingers.

It's easy to learn how to play with flying discs. They don't weigh much, so you don't have to be very big or strong to make them fly. I've seen very young children having fun with flying discs. Adults play with them, too. Some of the players are very good and compete in organized disc tournaments and games.

One adult player offered to teach Alex and me how to throw our discs better. His name is John, and he has competed in tournaments all over the world. He also gives demonstrations that show people how to improve their throwing and catching skills.

11

John suggested that we do exercises before we play. The exercises helped stretch our bodies and made them more limber. John said that our muscles should be loose and warmed up so that we'd avoid muscle pulls while running and jumping. John also showed us special exercises that would strengthen our wrists for throwing.

12

After we warmed up, John showed us the **backhand throw**. This is the most common throwing method, and it is very easy to learn. First John showed us how to **grip**, or hold, the disc. Your thumb is on top, and your index finger rests along the rim. The rest of your fingers firmly grip the bottom of the disc.

When your grip feels comfortable, you curl your wrist in as you draw your throwing arm across your body. Then you step in the direction you want the disc to travel, and you swing your arm forward. Release the disc with a snap of the wrist.

The **wrist snap** is very important. John said that your wrist should move just as if you were snapping a towel. A good wrist snap makes the disc spin very fast as it flies forward. The spin will help the disc fly straight and level without wobbling.

If you watch the disc carefully, it will sail right into your hand. The disc will be spinning very fast when you catch it. I keep my thumb up to stop the disc and let it settle right into the palm of my hand. You must remember to squeeze the disc tightly as you catch it. If you don't catch it firmly, it will spin right out of your fingers.

I really enjoy catching flying discs. But the hardest part for me is judging where the disc will come down. Sometimes I really have to run to catch long or high tosses before they hit the ground.

You can make the game more interesting by varying your catches. Sometimes you can keep your thumb down as you catch the disc. You can also catch it with two hands. The important thing is to make each catch cleanly so that you can throw quickly to another player. This keeps the disc moving and gives everybody many chances to throw and to catch.

You can also make the game more exciting by changing your throw to make the disc fly differently. You can make the disc curve, float, or skip simply by changing the angle it makes as you release it. If you tilt it sideways as you release it, the disc will curve to the right or to the left.

To make the disc skip, you tilt the front edge of the disc down as you step forward and snap your wrist. The disc will hit the ground and bounce up into the catcher's hands. This trick works best on hard surfaces like sidewalks or paved playgrounds.

My favorite throw is a **floater**. To throw
a floater, tilt the front edge of the disc up
as you release it. The disc will sail upward
and then stop and hover in front of the
catcher. The floater is a good throw for
advanced play.

My friends and I are always practicing
the basic backhand, the curve, the skip,
and the floater. It took us a long time to
be able to throw them correctly every time.
Many times the disc would sail in the
wrong direction or go too far. Then we had
to chase after it. But that was fun, too.

During our practice sessions, we began to learn how to use the wind to help our throws. The wind can carry your disc with it or help the disc return to you. Now we feel that the wind is our friend. We always check to see which way the wind is blowing by dropping a few blades of grass or some grains of sand and watching which way they scatter.

Later John showed us some other ways to throw our discs. One method is the **underhand throw**. You begin with the same grip you use for the backhand toss.

To deliver the throw, cock your wrist and swing the disc behind your hip. As you swing the disc forward again, step toward the target and plant your foot firmly. Release the disc with a snap of your wrist.

Another more advanced throw is called the **overhand** or **wrist flip**. You grip the disc as Alex does in these pictures. She puts her thumb on the bottom and rests her fingers on the rim. Then she cocks the disc back and releases it by snapping her whole arm forward. Alex can make the disc curve and skip using this throw.

You will need a lot of practice to master the wrist flip. But it is a very graceful toss and fun to use. Whenever I do the wrist flip I feel like an athlete throwing a discus!

Catching the disc is just as much fun as throwing it. John showed us some catches that look like tricks but are really simple to learn. You can catch low-flying discs between your legs. You can keep both feet on the ground or jump into the air. You can even catch the disc with your knees.

A catch **behind the back** looks very difficult. You need a good throw to make it work. Turn slightly and reach behind your back to grab the disc as it spins past. I like the feeling of catching the disc without seeing it, but I had to practice a lot to be able to judge where the disc would be. A **behind-the-head catch** is also very exciting.

A **fingertip catch** is a great way to catch a high floater. You stick out your index finger and touch the underside of the spinning disc. As the disc slows, your finger will move out toward the rim. If your timing is perfect, the disc will spin like a top on your fingertip.

Alex and I practice these catches together. We know that it is important for the thrower and catcher to communicate with each other. When Alex wants to try a fingertip catch, for instance, I will throw her a high floater.

When I want to practice catching the disc between my legs, Alex will throw me a straight low toss.

It's no fun throwing the disc over Alex's head or out of her reach on purpose. Then she can't practice catching it, and it takes longer for her to return the disc to me.

Alex and I discovered that we can play many different games with our flying discs. One game that is very popular is **golf**. Golf played with flying discs is very much like regular golf played with balls. The object is to hit a marked target, or **pole**, with as few throws as possible.

Alex and I played our first game of golf on a special course near our homes. The course had signs describing how to reach each target. We began throwing from a marker called a **tee**. Then we all took turns throwing our discs. We would mark where our discs landed and then make another throw from that spot.

COUNTY OF LOS ANGELES
Dept. of Parks & Recreation

FRISBEE GOLF COURSE

1. Frisbee is played like regular golf using a Frisbee. Frisbee etiquette will be maintained.

2. Tee area is within the rock circle or between the poles.

3. Each throw is scored as one stroke. A Frisbee out of reach, in a tree or bush, or out of bounds counts as an additional throw.
   (Park roads are out of bounds.)

4. The Frisbee must be thrown with one foot on the spot where the previous throw has landed.

5. A Frisbee hitting the Frishole pole constitutes successful completion of that hole.

6. The lowest score for previous hole will tee off first on the following hole.

7. The established Par for this course is 68. Each player keeps his own score.

8. Black signs indicate front 9. Red signs indicate back 9.

Happy Frisbeeing

When we got near a pole, accuracy became very important. Each player kept throwing until his or her disc hit the pole. If we threw too hard, our discs sometimes sailed way past the target. Once everyone had hit the pole, we again teed off on our way to the next pole.

Each player kept track of the number of throws it took to hit the target. I felt very good when I hit a pole in **par**. Par is the average number of tosses it takes to hit a pole.

If I took four tosses to hit a par-3 pole, that meant I threw one toss more than the average person. Alex was very good and usually threw fewer tosses than I did.

Parts of the golf course were very tricky. It had lots of trees, bushes, and hills. When one of our discs landed in a tree, the thrower was given a one-point penalty. As we walked along the golf course, we decided that we could easily set up our own course using utility poles, trees, or fence posts as targets.

Playing in the dirt and rough brush scratched and marred our flying discs. We cleaned them with soap and water. I also used light sandpaper to polish out the scratches on my disc. This makes the disc last longer and fly better, too.

Alex and I play another popular disc game at school. The game is called **ultimate**. It is a team sport similar to soccer. The object of the game is to pass the disc among your teammates until you cross a goal line and score.

We sometimes play other disc games called **guts** and **double disc court**. We liked to watch the older players practice these games, too. The guts players form two teams and try to throw their discs safely past the opposing players.

39

The players in double disc court try to land their discs on specially marked areas of the court before their opponents catch them.

Some people, like John, compete in flying disc tournaments. One tournament in my city is called the Beach Bowl. The biggest event is the **freestyle** contest. The freestyle competitors do a variety of tricks and difficult throws with their flying discs. They perform routines to music.

John and a partner competed as a freestyle team at the Beach Bowl I attended. I ran to the front to watch them perform. John made the disc spin on his head. He used his knees, elbows, and fingers to bounce and control the disc. He did very well, and I was really proud of him.

Later John showed my friends and me how to do some of the basic tricks used in freestyle events. John said the key is to use the disc's spinning motion to make your throws and actions as long as possible.

One way to keep the disc spinning is called **air brushing**. You cup your hand and then lightly strike the disc along its edge. If you face the wind while you brush, the disc will spin away from you for a moment, and then it will return.

Another freestyle trick is called **tipping**. It is similar to the fingertip catch. You place your index finger under the spinning disc and push it upward. The disc will rise off your finger and then settle back down until you tip it again. John uses a special spray lubricant to help make tipping easier. The spray covers the bottom of the disc with a slick surface.

John also showed us some body rolls. For this trick, the disc's spin helps it roll down one arm, across the chest, and up the other arm. Experts use many different parts of the body to roll the disc.

There are hundreds of games and tricks you can do with flying discs. Alex and I make up new ones all the time. She likes games where accuracy is important. I like performing tricks and special catches that I could use one day in freestyle contests. We both know that disc flying is for us!

FRISBEE® DISC FLYING Words

AIR BRUSHING: Striking or slapping the disc to control its motion

BACKHAND: A basic flying disc throw

BEHIND-THE-BACK CATCH: A blind catch made behind the back

BEHIND-THE-HEAD CATCH: A blind catch made behind the head

BODY ROLL: A freestyle trick in which the disc rolls along parts of the player's body

CURVE: A thrown disc that travels in an arc

GOLF: A disc game similar to ball or conventional golf

DOUBLE DISC COURT: A disc game played on a court by two-person teams

FINGERTIP CATCH: Catching the disc by placing the index finger on the disc's underside

FLIGHT PLATE: The top surface of a flying disc

FLIGHT RINGS: The concentric circles on the flight plate

FLOATER: A high throw in which the disc loses forward motion and seems to hover in the air

FREESTYLE: An event in flying disc competitions in which competitors perform tricks and disc control techniques to music

FRISBEE®: A brand name and a registered trademark of Wham-O Manufacturing Company

GUTS: A team game in which players try to throw a disc past their opponents

GRIP: The method of holding the flying disc

NOVELTY DISCS: Special-purpose flying disc toys

OVERHAND: Disc tosses made with a raised throwing arm

PAR: The average number of throws taken to hit a golf target

POLE: The goal or target in disc golf

RIM: The bottom edge of a flying disc

SHOULDER: The curved sides of a flying disc

SKIP: A throw that bounces off the ground surface

TEE: The starting place for each golf pole

TIPPING: Controlling the motion of a flying disc with your index finger or other parts of your body

ULTIMATE: A team game similar to soccer but played with flying discs

UNDERHAND: A backhand throw made from the same side of the body as the throwing arm

WRIST FLIP: One type of overhand throw

ABOUT THE AUTHOR/PHOTOGRAPHER

TOM MORAN is a freelance writer and the author of two photographic books. He has coached youth football, soccer, and boxing, and he frequently writes on sports subjects for California magazines and newspapers. Mr. Moran lives in Venice, California.